Camping with Aunt Julie

by Darlene Ramos
illustrated by David Harrington

Scott Foresman
is an imprint of

PEARSON

Glenview, Illinois • Boston, Massachusetts • Mesa, Arizona
Shoreview, Minnesota • Upper Saddle River, New Jersey

Illustrator David Harrington

Photographs
Every effort has been made to secure permission and provide appropriate credit for photographic material. The publisher deeply regrets any omission and pledges to correct errors called to its attention in subsequent editions.

Unless otherwise acknowledged, all photographs are the property of Pearson Education, Inc.

Photo locators denoted as follows: Top (T), Center (C), Bottom (B), Left (L), Right (R), Background (Bkgd)

16 Karl Kummels/SuperStock

ISBN 13: 978-0-328-39407-4
ISBN 10:   0-328-39407-6

7 8 9 10 V0FL 16 15 14 13

Aunt Julie loved to travel all over the world.
She didn't travel in comfort. She preferred
to camp out in jungles or hike up mountains
without the comforts of home.

Scott loved when Aunt Julie returned from her travels. She would open her book of photographs and tell exciting stories about the places she had visited. Then she'd give Scott his souvenir.

Tonight Scott held a beautiful piece of wood shaped like a shark. He felt the smooth wood and listened to Aunt Julie talk about an island far away.

Scott gazed at the pictures and imagined Aunt Julie swimming in a blue ocean full of yellow fish and a shiny shark.

Scott lived in a big city and did not travel much. He had an idea.

"Aunt Julie," Scott began, "do you think I could go on a trip with you some time?"

"Sure!" Aunt Julie answered. "I'm heading to the desert next week. Why don't you come with me?"

Scott looked at his parents. He was surprised when they didn't object. In fact, they didn't even blink!

When Aunt Julie pulled in the driveway, her van was filled with all kinds of camping things. She had sleeping bags, folding chairs, and small pots and pans.

"Are you ready to head west?" Aunt Julie asked.

"Let's go!" Scott said as he tossed his suitcase in the van.

Before the trip, Scott had a vision of his adventure. It included a soft bed, a television, and running water.

"So, Scott, do you know how to set up a tent?"

"A tent? Why do we need a tent?" Scott asked.

"Why, to sleep in!" Aunt Julie laughed. "The desert nights are cold!"

Scott was surprised. "We're sleeping in a tent? But, what about TV? I need to plug in my MP3 player!"

Aunt Julie just smiled and didn't reply. Scott felt trapped. The idea of living without his music and TV was like a prison sentence. It was punishment! That's why his parents didn't blink!

When the travelers finally arrived in the desert, Scott was a little worried. The desert was beautiful, but it was also strange and scary.

Aunt Julie started humming and setting up the tent.

"Do you want to help put up the tent?" she asked.

But Scott just sat on a rock listening to his MP3 player.

The battery was low. Soon the player would be useless for the rest of his term in the desert.

Just then a large animal flew very close to Scott's head.

Scott ducked. "What was that?" he asked fearfully.

"Oh, just a bat," Aunt Julie replied with a smile.

Scott jumped up and grabbed the tent. "So, how do we put this up?"

Later that evening, Aunt Julie built a small fire with the wood she had brought for fuel. She showed Scott how to roast marshmallows and told stories about desert animals and the stars.

"The desert is filled with sound," Aunt Julie explained. "It has its own music."

Scott sat quietly, listening to a few coyotes. He felt safe by the fire with his aunt. Then he realized why he liked her so much.

Aunt Julie lived life without needing a lot of things. She didn't need a TV or an MP3 player. All she needed was to travel and to spend time outside.

Suddenly, a strong gust of wind blew out
the fire, and a large owl flew past Scott. This
time Scott wasn't afraid.

"I'm lucky to have an aunt like you," he said.
"And, boy, will I have some stories to tell my
friends when I get home!"

The Desert at Night

Many desert animals are nocturnal. That means they sleep during the day when the desert is hot. At night, when the sun goes down, nocturnal animals come out to drink water and hunt for food. The sand and air are cool.

Some nocturnal desert animals are the bat, owl, and coyote. Bats feed on the nectar of cactus flowers. Owls eat desert mice or lizards. Coyotes hunt for mice and rabbits, but they also will eat reptiles.